Three Drops
of Chocolate

A Story by
Ramona Rodgers

**STRONG
PUBLISHING
House**

Bringing the strength of your words to reality

THREE DROPS OF
CHOCOLATE

A Story By Ramona Rodgers

Cover Photo: courtesy of *Jacorey C. Walker, Walker Productions*

Three Drops of Chocolate
By: Ramona Rodgers

Published by **Strong Publishing House**
Send all questions or inquiries to:
strongpublishinghouse@gmail.com

Acknowledgements

My writings are descriptive accounts of my growth into becoming a woman. I call this book "Three Drops of Chocolate" each drop representing the different moments in my life which account for my vision of my environment, personal journey, and the proclamation of my heritage as a Black Woman. I like to thank everyone I love, my grown #@! children, the wonderful babies, my mother, father, and ALL my siblings, friends and other family members (too many to name) and the species from "Mars". Without all of you…my "chocolate" would not exist.

Kiss, kiss

Contents

What's better than beauty

I do not consider myself beautiful

I consider myself to be "bountiful"!

My idea of beauty: being humorous, resourceful, and able to present a sexy swag to add to the wonderment of my "bountifulness".

I've seen beauty at its superficial realms, unmasking the ugly of fake hair, fake nails, fake lips and fake personalities to intertwine with this façade of beauty.

I smile at those who wish they knew the secrets of beauty, who glance, stare and wonder what magical spell I have spun. Such magnetic allure.

Beauty is bountiful!

Are you near

I want to see, and look at someone like me.
As I look around I don't see anyone reflecting me, my
characteristics, skin, hair, color or nose.
I wonder are they hiding, or lost trying to find me.
Searching, and lurking, why can't I see more of me
Bold like me
With smooth skin like me
Why are we less and few
Maybe being like "me" is hard to maintain, hard to find
Kinship from which I derive
My mirror is lonely it only reflects one
When two of me would multiply to many.

Uncertainty

At first glance, I noticed your smile, your way of dress.

I said to myself: "He's cute" and looked away.

Never had the desire to say "hello" to the opposite sex, at first sight-for fear of the unknown: Rejection. Ejection.

What's that like?

Embarrassment? A blow to the self-esteem? Or being placed in the center of male ridicule.

Ooooh, such a chilly thought. Then the table turns, where my eyes once devoured, is now looking back at me.

Something like Ike

I did not want the cake, but he did…

BAM! What was that for? Is this your way of professing your love to me?

To watch me on my hands and knees, crying, and begging please?

You are pulling my very soul out of me and my ancestry lineage is feeling my pain and is screaming for relief.

BAM! Not again! Where is this going…Not my head, I can't think, think, think…

Where are my shoes?

I said I didn't want the cake…

Gentleman talk

As I view, sit and listen I examine how he speaks.

I observe his hair, eyes, and formations of his mouth-to see how his thoughts flow with his verbal eloquence-how these words seem to "fit" his physical significance.

Impressive. Man of color.

Defying the spiritual writings of "Souls of Black Folks" by W.E.B Dubois

No longer looking "through the eyes of others"

Identifying yourself for who you are, a MAN shadowing no one.

Fuck Love

A game,

Over and over again, Love. Fuck Love!

Love got me.

Love made me cry, Love made me panic, Love made me sick.

Love made my head spin like Linda Blair in the movie *Exorcist*. Love made war. Love made Eve bite the fig, to test the love of a man. Fuck love!

Love? Love is what you get when you eat chocolate, Love is what you get when a baby smiles or when you take a hot bath to melt away impurities-Love is like juices in an orange running down your fingers, and dripping to your wrist leaving the sticky residue of flavor...That's Love.

Love? Love made me act crazy, Love made me stalk. Love made me scream! Shout! "What the fuck!" Love made me stupid, Love made me regret, Love made me wish for a new life again! Love stole my heart, Love ran from me, Love whispered in my ear and said, "I won't hurt you" you mean the world to me... See, Love lies too.

Fuck Love!

Zoo Life

Petty thief-
High life. Living high. Glam life

On the pleasure of someone else their sweat perhaps even
tears.

Y?

To satisfy the demon within yourself
A friend, or maybe even a worthless man.

When fun was out of sight

Streets
Was a fun place to be.
At least when I was young and small
Freeze tag, red-light-green light, innocent tricks on friends,
collard greens, cornbread, white beans, Mr. frosty and
frozen ice cubes-
Chuck Taylor high tops in black n white
Everything was groovy and cool now, that's all
right what's going down! Give me 5, I'm hip, you just full
of jive!
Bell bottoms, knee socks, stripped and solid-hula
hoops, jacks and spinning tops-how could I forget the afros
shining with afro sheen-soul train popping, bouncing and
dancing to the "love machine"
Woolworth, and Kresgees, and Montgomery wards
Buy me a piece of candy–Maryjanes if you please-give me
20 and also 1 piece of bubblegum-Sugar Daddys with Red
Hot Dollars, along with Boston Baked Beans. And for my
bestest friend she only wants 4.

Take me to the next phase baby take me!
The Jackson 5, the Silvers, and Osmonds (yes the Osmonds
too), I'm just taking it back to the old school-men wore half
shirts and the boys did too with flying tails on shorts
Everybody, everybody in yes, yes we all jump in! We did
the hustle to begin the bump especially when Big Butt
Bertha began to rump
Michael Jackson was Off The Wall
Prince was doing his baby

Shoot our lives was grand living together hand in hand
But now my good people I must take you somewhere
else…to our new reality on the street
Nigga get off my block!
That's what you hear when the block is hot
What?
Man bump you, you ain't nothing but a punk
Watcha' gon do?

Watsup man? (Bam) your gone, don't get it twisted the
young sisters are just as wicked, cussing, fussing,
stabbing, and jabbing, daring a young brotha to even
jump at 'er!
See, these girls are tough like Glad trash bags built like
Mac trucks able to withstand a lot of stuff-
Nails done,
Hair did,
Babies on the hip watcha mean don't trip
I am trying to figure out what is with the madness
clearly there must be a reason why our streets have
changed our children, is it the water is it the food or is it
payback for the things grown folks didn't do….

Malcolm X once said, "We have a hard enough time in
our own struggle for justice and already have enough
enemies as it is to make a drastic mistake of attacking
each other and adding more weight to an already
unbearable load."

When will we learn?

Jungle

Our lives and streets are surrounded by jungle-species unknown.
Half-man, Half–animal
Combined is a bipolar catastrophe! Does his soul tell him to prey on the naïve, or does his mind tell him to preserve nature!
Does he continue to make war-topple down on the weakest being?
He transforms his gods, his beliefs, his wisdom to worlds untouched by violence, or greed
He brings
Havoc,
Fear,
Inhibitions of self–love
A jungle.
Who is responsible beast or man.
Can he regain his M-A-N stature
Or will he hold on to the Dr. Hyde, Mr. Jekyll Syndrome for life
Man was not placed on earth to eliminate, annihilate, or violate.
The question, whether Man or Beast prevails.
History is the answer.

The day the Ghetto came home

You've arrived. So happy you came home. What? "You is too?" "Well, sit down, rest yourself, glad to know you are here to represent "Today's Mentality."

Yes, sir! You are our big lottery winner! Mr. Rufus Lemar–Renaldo Hashuan Green. You don't appear to be the type that sits around and expect the world to bow down at his feet. Nor, do you appear to be the type who would "blow" my head off if I stepped on your new Jordan's. "What?" Well, probably-but, I guess we would both be dead, "huh?" you don't care? What do you mean? "Cuz" What, you do or die? You got your entourage, your boys? "Humph." Is this your girl? Well, hello, Ms. Ahh, Ms. Tanqueray. "Oh, your mama named you Tanqueray?" I, see, "Cuzzin she love dat drank!" I am not trying to make fun of anyone. Yes, we can get down to business. I hope you read the fine print also in the rules and regulations we mailed to you. Good, good. "Well, you realize that half of your lottery proceeds have to go back to your community." What do you mean, what? You said you read the rules and regulations. Sir, Ma'am, down please! Let me explain. It is your choice where the money will go, but, may I make a few suggestions? Your, quite welcome, don't thank me, flatter me.

Start, with the Mothers and Fathers who allowed children to see violence, and ugliness and not deter their "very own" from committing such acts. Next, a portion of winnings need to go to preschools for children to be "deprogrammed" from name brand clothes, explicit videos and movies, you know, just to start all over again, "basic colors, for basic parents, who never taught their child basic education." Go, back and look at the neighborhoods see how homes are abandoned, condemned, or vandalized. Think, about reopening youth centers, beautifying parks, and playgrounds, just so you can reminisce about your childhood, you know, to hear the echoing sounds of children's laughter. It would not hurt for you to consider elementary schools and high schools. Start with "Dick and Jane" readings, one-step division, and multiplication facts, "cultural history" anything to help our youth, nothing a little money can't do. "What?" you refuse to give, well the fine print did clearly state as follows: "As payee of the lottery it is a requirement for all winners to give ½ of winnings to their communities" Sir, you must honor your rules as payee or you will forfeit the winnings. Sir, you were not tricked, fooled, or bamboozled, one must give to get! One must read, one must learn, one must expect the unexpected, if he is to shed himself of the selfish, violent, womanizing labels that society has given him! It is your choice! Your decision! It is totally up to you! To change the image! It is up to you, to decide what a "million" bucks can do for you.

Speak of history

Significant. Established. Heritage.

From the sands and shores of Africa to the red dirt of
Alabama
History began to speak…

History spoke when the "New Man" discovered our land of
freedom and cast their weapons of captivity

History spoke when feet of blackness touched the grounds
of America.

History spoke when Big Mama's herbs and spices were
smelled across the plantation coming from the Massa's
kitchen.

History spoke when our great, great, great, greatness of
grandfather's opened a book and read by candlelight.

History spoke when the field hands worked from sun up to
sun down yet, not treated better than livestock kept in
barns.   Were our Ancestors man made machines?

History spoke when men and women sang songs of
Homeland not forgetting from whence they came.

History spoke when man and woman jumped the broom
and produced more generations to be self-proclaimed!

History spoke when the day of freedom finally came true!

History spoke when Angela Davis wore a dynamic afro!

History spoke when Malcolm X gave up his pimp hat to speak against racial injustice and fight for empowerment!

History spoke when Jackie Robinson crossed that professional sports color line!

History spoke to Decatur when Broadway Street became Martin Luther King!

History has spoken to me and I am speaking to you by which my words are delivered through poetry. History will continue to speak as long as Black People Exist for our history is much deeper than what the history books suggest.

Our Voice

Can you hear the sound, Can you feel the rhythms can you imagine? Just Imagine…
As I take you on a journey…..of music, live music, real music, music which make your dreams a reality, and your body sway and swing like branches on a sycamore tree

Mahalia Jackson,
Miles Davis,
Billie Holiday,
Charlie Parker, flow, flow, blow, blow, give me the beat withstanding the heat, natural flow, candle lights glisten, as you relax and listen-
Now today the music has a little mo' flava
Hard, loud, upbeat, proud lyrics usually leaving my hearing in a craze, but still music nonetheless to the youth now daze, from Tupac, to Mike Jones, to Lil Wayne, words that sometimes have profound meaning, describing what it's like
To be heard but not seen as a young black youth without recognition unless of "bling-bling" ambition
To show how much we love to live, and live to love give back with the voice-
Rather it soft, loud, hard, or rough!

Flow, flow, blow, blow
Our song in one voice

Just aching to be heard
As WE Mellow the world.

Natural Musicians

Hear the backbeats of the drums, as you replace them with
the pounds of your hands
Only the beats from your head, only the rhythms of your
heart-why is your music

Making
You dance
Alone

$\mathscr{I}$ tried to say my peace without causing confusion

Don't Go…

I tried hard to say my peace without causing confusion-it was misconstrued and became a problem.

I ran upon a situation where I was placed between a choice of drowning or smashing into a concrete wall-not even the most aggressive person could escape such an empowering pull to "gasp" for breath to exhale.

Even though we communicated and expressed emotional concern my heart never skipped a second beat-it only echoed from whence was.

I still hear laughter, I still see the smiles, but I have to ask myself, is it all worthwhile. I do not want to go through, what if's, why not's, or should have been. I only want what is now.

Attempting not to be alarmed by the sudden crying game I've caused, leading to ill feelings and resentment, down from deep within, I want to beg for forgiveness not because I am ashamed, but because I never knew pain could exist in a body of salt, like yours.

I try to contemplate on how soon I could run or break away like the wind blowing diamond dust bedazzling everyone with its new coming out song, only real hearts can hear, but a strong force keeps bringing me back again, is it the turbulence from my heart, or the origins of my mind, either way, I try to refrain from looking back, it's hard.

"To be, or not to be," is certainly the question. I just wonder if Shakespeare ever found the answer, or shall I.

Get Him
(MY VALENTINE THAT IS)

Valentine,
Where are you? Cupid told me he was going to work
overtime.

Did you dodge his arrows? Or maybe have on an armored
vest?
Did it rain and you were able to avoid the love dust? You
must have cause I ain't seen a sign that says, "Marry me or
Bust"

Valentine, my vase is empty, I see no "be mine" balloons,
my lingerie is tearing from lack of use!
Could you please stand still for a least one minute, and let
the arrow hit you in the spot that's tight and round, so cupid
can report you did scream my name "out loud!"

The love doctor is tired of flying, tired of trying-
Cupid said to me, "Shoot he's fast!" my arrows won't even
hit the bottom of his feet! He was running and jumping
over cars, like he was a collegiate runner in an all-star track
meet!

Now, don't get it wrong this is not desperation it's just that
a woman like me feels you should give in without
hesitation!
I'm praying, doing little stalking-
Oh, by the way is that a picture of your mother on the north
side of the wall? Cause if it is, you don't look like her at
all!

Valentine, come on give a girl a chance, maybe if you are lucky you will get a little dance….

Cupid has given up, my heart is aching, I guess this is a sign that all good men are taken.
So, on Valentine's Day I guess I will be alone again…But, hold up wait a minute, don't look now, there is your fine "hot" friend, "come on cupid we got work to do!"
Here is my chance to find another "Boo".

Happy Valentine's Day!

(This poem is not written to make fun of women. Just something "sweet" and funny to make your day "SMILE")

Cccccopulation

Tasting sweet, candy is like enjoying S-E-X
Melting chocolates, Position 69, at your place or mine-
Succulent strawberries dipped in mint, heavy breathing,
bodies intertwined.
Wine me dine me, take me on all fours
You like edible undies? Poppin' grape's my favorite what's
yours?
Sucking on fingers, lobes, and breast honey poured all over
my ample chest.
Sheets in satin, oils in mystic blue, candle fragrance smells
of "Sex Island II"
"Do me baby" in Prince's words
I want to reach a climax that takes me to the peak of Mt.
Everest
Reaching an orgasm as if I have just combusted!

>   As
>   I
>   Climb
>   Down

From such a thrill
I want to try again…but this time I want to be a nurse, and
you an injured soldier with a big gun…let the war games
began.

All different

All different.   All the same
What exactly is in a name?
Of course, there are syllables to begin
With Latin and Greek origins to extend
We are given names to represent our culture like
Rashaad, Pookie, Yhahna, Slim or Red along with Breann,
Kontel and 'Lil' man!
So, careful how you identify words meaning destruction or
negative connotations. For, representing your name can
declare separation. Don't signify segregation within your
own race. What was the point of Freedom Riders, Martin
or Rosa Parks? They did not represent the civil rights thug
bus!

Youth now cry for power only to be gained by nonsense
and violence! Who associate themselves with "Squad"
names to be acknowledged?
What happened to "I have a Dream" to "Keep Hope Alive",
"By any means Necessary"?
Our kids hear this and scratch their heads and say, "Dat
Der', wat dat mean" turning back to the faces of slave
mentality.
I shake my head, hide, and duck and declare out loud,
"OUR KIDS ARE TRULY Struck!"

Heart of a so called gangsta

I am like a child in a womb waiting to be held in his
mother's arms
Like a toddler-son who jumps, pulls, and breaks items
waiting to be chastised by loving hands

An elementary kid popping rubber bands in the classroom,
playing B-ball with the boys, and pulling girls hair, while
knocking them down...in the principal's office with a look
of defeat waiting on mom to come and rescue me.

A teenage boy learning the rites of passage to manhood
waiting for my Dad to shake my hand, with a loving
embrace...

A grown man now becoming a father, seeking friendship
and love from women not knowing my manhood and love
was never developed–love was never granted or fully
delivered to me, how, can I give my heart, it aches and
seeks fulfillment

Really...

I am an old man now, reminiscing on the days, of what was,
I am not old because of old age, but old-time has been
draining me and pulling me like a mule with his plow
A man trying to define what it is to be a man...and it has to
be real...this time

What's my name

Who am I?
I did not catch those words you have spoken to me so
strongly

YOU SAID I AM A
Jigga Boo?
Niglet?
Mamie, Nigger?
Coon, Moon Cricket, Uncle Tom, Nigra, Porch Monkey?
Darky, Blackie, Tar Baby, Spook?
House Nigga, Bitch?
Cotton picking jungle bunny? Sell out Honkey lover?

I am who and what I am but let it be known. You cannot
beat or break this foundation of me.

Creation of this…?

Ingenious,
Such a wonderful sight.
A pleasant view for the imagination
A thought a monumental explosion…Love.

Leaving the world

I never had thoughts of suicide

I always felt God was touching my shoulders, he gave me hindsight to see beyond instant moments of condemnation. People who cast their lives away as such has left behind a trail of broken hearts and tears of wondering, Why?

Suicide does not have to mean "death"

It could be described as time exhausted, wasted or procrastinated due to mindless feelings of alienation.

Who can reach deep in one's soul and scathe through a mind so discombobulated to discourage such a betraying act of self-appraisal which was needed on earth while flesh was present.

Suicide is now a game plagued by media attention to make assumptions and instant conclusions of why death or deaths has occurred by an individual or individuals who take lives and leave others with

Endless pain
Endless suffering
Endless guilt,

Burial sights to be visited upon holidays or empty days still seeking answers

Suicide is life, when the majority changes the rules and you fight your plea for equality

Suicide is making the wrong choice in life and the latter part should have been decided

Suicide is allowing others to predict your future.

Craze

Do not make my world a living hell when you know how I will react!
Do not tell me what I can do!

If your world is circling around a brain with uncontrollable thoughts which flip you in a box of bias!

Do not try to change me from which I was conceived.
Who asked you to disturb my crrrrraze!

Where should I be

My foundation has yet to be discovered. I want the nature of love to be unselfish, but I have reservations…which will not allow me to give freely like the love of a baby, a sweet gentle baby who "smiles" because of the quiet kisses sent by an angel to keep her innocence.

I am torn between my worldly thoughts and my golden heart

When will my journey end?

Talk to me about my beauty

Talk to me about my beauty…
Beauty is wonderful in so many ways, but, it happens to be
"Black".
Black is just, me, you, your sons and daughters, in the seed
of our souls
To the tip of toes
To the tingling of fingers
To the vision of "my" world
To you my beauty is only what you see…and what you
feel, but my beauty is black
…Isn't this why black is beautiful?

Lost as they say

People say I need Jesus
Do I not recognize the side that can save my soul?
I do, and Jesus is by my side
I am a purpose, and I am still here
…A never ending story of the state of being.

Do I

A lady such as myself, angry
Lady such as myself, different
Lady such as myself, strong
Lady such as myself wants to grow
A lady such as myself feels her life is not complete
Lady such as me?...A diaspora of greatness when the forces
are unbearable to sustain
But, yet do I react to
Negativity?
Criticism?
Snide remarks?
Or do I project the dignified look and act as if your
presence does not exist in my mirror, there is no reflection
of you in what I do and say.
So why do I feel captured by resentment...because what I
see is ME.

𝒟ecipher

BLACK WOMAN STANDING.
Respect me. Question me. Love me. Walk with me.
Teach me.
If my aura is smooth and cool allow me to move on.   I am
maintaining my foundation to remain uplifted.
RESPECT ME.
If my habits, gestures, or appearance is unbearable for the
public eye to witness, kindly guide me, address me
accordingly, as not to ignite a flame to form a fire.
QUESTION ME.
Gentlemen, if you just so happen to lose your swagger and
your backbones soften like jelly, allow nurturing hands, and
impeccable minds with swaying hips to stand strong on
your ground.
LOVE ME.
If I am losing sight of why my plight to exist is relevant to
the masses around me, remind me, I groove better when I
know I'm in charge.
TEACH ME.
If I refuse to bow down to issues concerning ill treatment of
women, allow me to roar in a paramount nature, in order to
be heard.
WALK WITH ME.
See, as a woman I should not have to stand on my head, or
scream, or holler to amplify my existence. You should
already know I am here, trust enough to know.
Appearing before you and for you is an ingenious, earthly,
exuberant, stupendous, melodic flower empowered to
bloom for centuries to come…can YOU decipher this?

Secret Visitor

Who blew in the cold mass of air causing a shadow of blues over my body?
Can you creep in quietly?
Warm me? Start at my stem extend to my branches and touch me ever so lightly?
MMMMMMMM, our heat is soothing like sweet honey dripping in tea. I arch my back as you warm my inner loins.
I love when you greet me
I hate when you leave me
My friends gaze at me with envy and say "Girl what's his name?"
I smile and respond "Putntang"
I anticipate to come, as I toss, turn, moan, groan. I want to scream-I can't my neighbors will hear
Please, Mr. Come, come into my mounds of
Cold darkness as I open my cave, I move quickly as you enter and I say:
Mr. Sun, where have you been I've waited for your rays of sunshine all night long.

Brain

In my head
      Grateful
            Sinful. Hateful.
                      Delightful
                      Beautiful words
                      Describing everything
                      rolled up in a day of one's
                      character

Good u feel…u feel good

As I awake from the morning sounds, I am exuberant, just
knowing I am alive-It's a new day!
I can start again, and again, you are a smile, a thought, a
continuance, a precedence, a conclusion, a title.
A book sitting in dust-Author Unknown, bursting from
words similar to students challenged in a spelling bee
whose mind is racing from A to Z.
But I've uncovered u, a masterpiece a vintage wine so
"fine" you make snakes lose their slither, and Stella
redefine her groove.
Good u feel, a real book, a classic only to be told by those
who have discovered your private chambers
U feel good
Your disposition is untouched, only when the goodness of
reading, shall anyone realize what it's like to touch the
cover of your book.

Epitome

The greatness of you and me
I exist in you, you exist in me
Wonderful is what I say, wonderful is what you be to me,
My epitome
What would my world be like if the greatness you bring left
me
Think about the epitome of beauty: trees, sun, the moon and
stars…you, me, he, she.
This is my epitome of wonder
What exactly is yours?

Arrival

The day you stirred within u were a God-given beauty, pure
life.
Drops of rain
Quietness of snow
Starlight shinning on my skin
Precious, Precious
Skin so soft, smell brand new, colors of life-
Brown, caramel, chocolate, and nutmeg brew
Commodity of love, treasure of hearts
Perfect little label, bundle of passion
Gathered by strands—one of woman and parts of man
Amazement, joy, special moments to reflect of what love
should project
During the breath of awakening.

Swish & Assist (Ode to Basketball)

I see you on the court,
Your smile
Your style
A look of determination,
Equal to frustration
Red face,
Bold face,
Game face,
"Mommies' baby face"
Play to win, win to play
…Basketball is so much better than boys

Rainbow of Chocolate

Take a look at yourself, what do you see?
I see pretty brown, brown
Look at yourself! It's alright, slowly turn your head around
and tell me what do you see?
Do you see?
Beautiful smooth mocha skin, caramel delight tones, rich
whipped almond glow, appearing to blend like waves in the
ocean to be greeted by the sea?
Look, look at yourself, what do you see? Hair, Hair in
different colors of black, burgundy, brown which is kinky,
coarse, straight or nappy, easy to touch, twist and pull into
different styles of wonder.
STOP! Stare yourself down, tell me what do you see?
Do you see?
Curves of wonder, pretty brown-brown, eyes of curiosity,
lips of thickness, hands of power, legs of steel, backbones
of endless strength? Designed, presented, and bequeathed
to you to affirm graciously.
Now walk, that walk like your existence has no bounds,
hold your head high like reaching for a new universe of
stars.
Now turn around, and ask yourself
What do I see?
Different hues of black and brown skin
Living and learning and blossoming together with
determination and a never ending legacy, intertwined in one
rainbow of chocolate

Miss Ramona Rodgers

Miss Ramona Rodgers, known for her witty and outgoing personality, is a native of Decatur, IL. She holds a Bachelors of Arts degree in Sociology/Anthropology and currently pursuing her Master's Degree in Cultural Education. She enjoys spending time with her family and friends, travelling, and of course writing. She is the founder of a girls group "US (Undeniably Smart) Girls" which focuses on building the character, self-esteem, and self-worth of young ladies. She is currently working on a children's book entitled: "My Daddy's Hands" to be published in the winter of 2013.

If you would like to order more copies of this book or other publications, please contact Strong Publishing House via email at strongpublishinghouse@gmail.com or visit our website at strongpublishinghouse.weebly.com

www.ingramcontent.com/pod-product-compliance
Lightning Source LLC
Chambersburg PA
CBHW071744020426
42331CB00008B/2171